AF303881

Verlag: BoD · Books on Demand GmbH, In de Tarpen 42, 22848 Norderstedt, bod@bod.de
Druck: Libri Plureos GmbH, Friedensallee 273, 22763 Hamburg

ISBN: 978-3-7693-1365-9

Inhalt

The Onset of October

'Round the onset of October
With the lifting of the heat's
Heavy pressure on my mind
Replaced as rain on rooftops beats
Lift the peoples' expectations
Summer, sun, a constant smile
Fin'lly let me start the sorting
Of what's long become a pile
Breeze of cold, a teardrop falling
Sink in duvets, two and three
Drink hot cocoa, start to sniffle
Let emotions now run free

Chestnuts, couches, candlelight

Back from walk, from boot to loafer
Chestnuts fill my pouch
Later friends are coming over
Cuddles on the couch
Candlelight and comfy sweaters
Oatmilk cocoa steam
Feet up, book in hand, the letters
Dance into a dream

Teacups held through sleeves like mittens
O'er the rim you grin
Just like me by fall you're smitten
And so my heart you win

Autumn Orange

In autumn orange, warm and bright
I show my hand, you hold it tight
A weight is lifted, lungs are freed
Uncertain, still, where this may lead
In citrus, mint, and ginger air
A step is taken, fine and fair
More safely I will never sink
So let I go of brim and brink
In autumn ev'ning, brisk and dim
I hold your hand, lean back and swim

Evening cold

took a step into the ev'ning
yellow streetlights, leaves that drip
autumn crystallized my breathing
froze my fingers, dried my lip
yet I smile into the darkness
as the cold my nose tip numbs
in unpleasantness my lark is
thoughts of you warm up my lungs

Place set in my heart

there's a place set in my heart
with your name writt' on a card
there's a plate, a salad bowl
fork and knife in napkin roll
there's a glass and there's a mug
choices what to sip or chug
and for when we want retire
know your chair here by the fire
has a blanket just for you
cozy socks and pillows, too
and upstairs then in the bathroom
there's a toothbrush and a cup
and a towel if you want to
take a shower, use the tub
and when fin'lly it's decided
it is time to go to rest
pillows, blankets, all provided
for my darling all the best

merry be who may

There on my calendar appear
The holidays I've come to fear
A season once highly revered
But children's wonder 's disappeared
Now joy 's replaced by a tensed-up neck
Once-home now a forgotten wreck
Festivities for families
Dust-covered deep in memories

freshest snow

dishes washed, the smell of lunch
how I feel? don't have a hunch
skipping shuffle, shards of songs
all of them, it seems, are wrongs
shovel sounds outside the window
purplish light from freshest snow

Alone

The day was good, the ev'ning fine
But in the darkness I'm alone
The only sound: a heartbeat, mine
Nobody hears my cry, my moan
It's me, afraid of nothingness
Alone with that itself
Nothing to see but shadows' mess
Nothing to hear but self
Nothing to feel but cloth and skin
Nothing to taste but spit
Nothing to smell but sweat within
This sad and hollow pit.

mushroom, cream and white wine

mushroom, cream and white wine
you and me at night time
this could be my lifeline
dinner had in bed

snow

three women build a snowman
law students in snowball fight
children in us all
in the glowy snowy white

Eternal Flower

The blossoming inside my chest
Commencing in the days
That Winter's frost is lain to rest
Replaced by warming rays
It is the remnants of a Garden
Of once eternal scope
A flower planted in my being
Still eternal: Hope

The weather in May

the weather in May
may change my way
I'm hoping that it might
for even now
I notice how
I'm lifted by the light

Summer Night

There are no words that, known to me,
Can tell of my desire
My longing, yearning, needing, how
My soul is set on fire

I close my eyes and I am there
With you and you beside me
A picture that, if prayers be heard,
Comes true this summer - maybe

The sunset over river's edge
Behind the skyline's shadow
A walk across the bridge to find
The destination meadow

The drinks are passed around, the same
With jackets, snacks and stories
And with the soft night wind are blown
Away all of our worries

Field trips for more food and drinks
Return to find us dancing
Sing-alongs to boom box sound
Not missing flirty glancing

To let the deep-talks blossom full
The box's volume lessened
The tales that told profound and true,
Tear-jerking and confessend

Guitars unpacked are joined with voices
Chords in throats, on strings
Mix and match, a chorus concert
Beautifully rings

Leaning back on cloth, dirt, grass I
Rediscover stars
Dive and sink - oh let me drown
In what right now is ours

Leave eyes closed
Yes, let this linger
Do not let the truth-thought bringer
In for just a minute longer
Longingly the dream grows stronger

Close your eyes and sink with me
Sing till it's reality

Italy in August

on the tram close to a heatstroke
when my headphones play your song
sing of italy in august
I could listen hours long
and your voice it calms my breathing
as I sink into my seat
and a smile not seen by strangers
on my masked lips I let creep

Open Eyes

open eyes, I see them laughing
no, I don't hallucinate
yes, we're here, it's real we're passing
stories as we celebrate

open eyes and them beside me
no, not all, but oh how grand
all this love I've been compiling
here it is and here I land

Cloudy Monday Afternoon

Weekend is over, new fam'ly departs
Hugs like exchanges of pieces of hearts
How do I cope now and what do I do
With my cloudy Monday afternoon

Tea forgotten in my sink
Since I made it just a blink
Still my room, still my apartment
Home has left with the departed

Was it really just a weekend?
Just a leap three days gone by
How 'm I meant to let that seep and
Let that sink into my mind?

a storm, my lover

the wind plays with the roofing tiles
and whistles past your window
it underscores our goofy smiles
then covers up our sin - oh -
our bodies move under your roof
with nothing else as cover
thus feeling you, don't need more proof
you are a storm, my lover

Clouds pass overhead

With you I'd watch the tide run out
And back onto the sand
I'd watch the clouds pass overhead
See kites fly high and land
Don't need a word passed 'tween our lips
No hand of yours in mine
Just know that in those moments' time
My heart it will be thine

How quickly I forget

A space between my chest and yours
Minute and minuscule
Exhausted bodies, voices hoarse
But laughter grants us fuel

Sunlight hits the rushing river
Just before its source will set
Grab a jacket for your shiver
Lines exchanged in slow duet

Running through a forest hillside
Lungs with laughter light
Never wordless, never quill-dried
With your ink on white

–

Oh, how quickly I forget
The times I don't wish back
The times in which I didn't know –
I did not love you yet

Touch the grass

Want to go back to that ev'ning,
Touch the grass and smell the air
Why does time always mean leaving?
Why does past come with a "where?"

Evergreens

A storm took all the conifers
They try to grow them back
For now, though, bald spots mark the hills
And underscore the lack
The only evergreen that's left
Are the hollies on the peak
Far up from all my favourite spots
Down by my favourite creek

Love like earth

I love you like I love the earth
A beauty known to end
But till it does, I'll show my love
By way of time I spend
So take it as we tell our tales
Of future and of past
And look with me at trees and dreams
We know will never last

Wild thyme

Wild thyme, wild time
Evergreen and never mine
Lilac summer, rare – bright
Stay the winter, stay the night

Winter's old deterioration

Winter's old deterioration
Has begun to take its toll
Hope for quick amelioration
Lies in dice I cannot roll
Twice it's come now, forces heavy
Taxes levied paid in joy
But for you my armor's ready
Yes for you I'll brave its ploy

To see the rain

You know the ways to see the rain
It's cleansing pain and putting strain
On tired nerves, I try to swerve
But in vain

And, yes I know you know the snow
The piles that grow, the smell of dough
And that of tea, I try to be
Not so low

You tell me "dance!", I take the chance
As if in trance, I take your hands
I see the rain, I see the snow
And know you know

I no longer dread the Darkness

I no longer dread the darkness
I just let it come and roll
Play its usual charade
I let it sink and take its toll
'Stead of dread, a tired welcome
"You again? Well, go ahead"
Like you deal with autumn ending
And with the time you go to bed
'Tis a thing that has its placement
In the rhythm of my life
I simply let it take me over
Do not rise to stand in strife
This might sound, to you, depressing
Reading this might strain or sting
But remember, dear, the morning
The returning of the spring

Through condensation

I watch through condensation
The dewy flowers wake
Us all in expectation
The grasp of winter shake

Sun rays

like sun rays just before the rise
dawn still softly dozing
pre the praise and posing
caref'lly lifted guise
just like that I aim to love you
just enough you'll find
wise and strong and kind

The Month of Mars

Whoever named the month of march
Cannot have payed attention
For who would see the birth of spring
And think about contention
Who would see the sun rise sooner
Spend more warming light
And think of spears and swords in bodies
Shivering with fright
Who would, seeing flowers grow
From meadows, think of mud
Battlefields by soldiers stomped
A war god drenched in blood

Where God is

I don't know who, what, where god is
But if they are in energy
Then forget 'bout being modest
They are here in you and me
I don't know if they are watching
But if they see your every part
They must see the way you're notching
Your initials in my heart

Do they see your hair cascading
O'er my arm and chest and face
As the sunset red is fading
At a sleep-inducing pace

They are there in what I'm feeling
As you're sleeping in my arm
Stars now start to spot our ceiling
Warmth is spread and breathing calm
It's the only explanation:
They are there within this love
In this beautiful sensation
Not just watching from above

River Bank

Just enough delirious
Drawing in the curious
"Let's keep walking", stay this high
Watch you spin, spin, spin and fly
Warmth has settled 'neath my skin
"To the bank?" asked with a grin
Feel the wind without a shiver
Watch how low and calm the river
Watch how fiéry your look
"Wanna find a quiet nook?"

And we do, just for us two
Limbs entangled, tender sighs
Watched by only mother moon
Stay until the sun will rise

Narcissus

You joke I'll die like Narcissus
Entranced by my reflection
Ironic 'bout remarks like this:
Just you invoke such action

I looked at you and in a dither
I couldn't speak nor move
So if transfixed, like him I'll wither
Those flowers are for you

September songs

Campfires and orange candles
List'ning to September Songs
Blankets wrapped 'round, mugs 'thout handles
Nights like this can right all wrongs

Earth's Pull

Lying on soft forest ground
Drifting still, yet feeling found
Amber rays through softwood trees
Answer to my unheard pleas
Brown of soil and green of moss
Discovery through death and loss
Getting up, I feel earth's pull
And tell her she is beautiful

light as autumn air

soul as light as autumn air
right after the rain
breathing out each worry, weary
breathing out each pain
watch the droplets – falling – flying –
wash it down the stream
river at my feet I'm sighing
I feel light and clean